PRAISE FOR THE CHRISTMAS GIFT

"The Christmas Gift brims with love and warmth…reminding us that miracles are indeed possible."

~Jane Choate, RWA author of Keeping Watch, Harlequin LI

PRAISE FOR JOURNEY TO SAND CASTLE

An unimaginable tragedy. Three broken lives. One more chance.

"Leslee Breene confronts conflict, resistance, and prejudice…in a well-written story of love and redemption."

~Heidi M.Thomas, WWW WILLA Literary Award Winner

"A tender story of love, family and healing, set in the Colorado San Luis Valley, Journey to Sand Castle is a wonderful addition to author Leslee Breene's previous novel publications."

~ Julie Simpson, www.ColoradocountryLife.coop

ALSO BY LESLEE BREENE

Journey to Sand Castle

Starlight Rescue

Hearts on the Wind

Leadville Lady

Foxfire

Anja!
Keep Christmas
in your heart!
Enjoy! Leslee
Breene

Christmas in My Heart

A Short Story Collection

Leslee Breene

DEDICATION

For Terry, soul mate and loving companion. And for
my nephew Lucas, and my grandnephews Witt and
Jaxon. Wishing you the true spirit of Christmas.

AUTHOR'S NOTE

From the beginning of my writing journey, I have always loved short stories. Literary mentors were Somerset Maugham, Eudora Welty, and Ernest Hemingway, to name a few. I am grateful to the former National Writers' Club and Rocky Mountain Fiction Writers for guiding, inspiring and compelling me to learn the craft in those early critique sessions.

The four short stories included in this collection are my tribute to Christmas—that most special holiday of the year. I invite you, the reader, to find a quiet place, filled with warmth and light, and immerse yourself in the characters and their lives, and hope each story will bring you an inner satisfaction. Or, make you recall a happy holiday memory in your own life's story.

At this Christmas may you and yours find love, joy and peace in your hearts.

Leslee Breene

CONTENTS

THE CARETAKER

November 1875: Buffalo River, Minnesota

"We can take no chances, Lars. We have to get Nellie into the house!" With the gust of a stormy night whipping up her skirt, Mama stands over our sick cow. She pulls her heavy woolen shawl closer around her large belly.

Papa strokes Nellie's head, a worrisome look spreading across his face above his full beard. "You want to bring her in the house, Sigrie?"

"Her calf will be born before morning and it will freeze in this bitter night," says Mama.

I shift from one foot to another, knowing Mama would never tell Papa what to do, but this is her job in our family. She is the *budeie*, the caretaker of cattle, and like the other women in our community, she takes it seriously.

Papa nods in agreement and peers up at the thin layer of slough grass covering the pole shed. The roof started as a thick layer last fall, but our cows have slipped their long, rough tongues between the poles many times for a lick and sometimes come away with mouthfuls.

"Selma, go put some salt in a pan and bring it here," Mama says. "And be quick about it!"

My youngest brother Carl and I run to our small log house, his short legs almost catching up to mine.

By the time I find the salt and put it in a pan, my oldest brother Jens has unloaded a stack of firewood near the stove. I order him to watch Carl and bolt outside into the whirling snow.

Papa has a rope around Nellie's neck. Together, the three of us coax her across the yard by holding the salt pan under her nose. Once through the front door, we shove the poor cow into my room and tie her to the bed post. Nellie and my bed fill the small room. Papa can barely get the door shut.

We hear her bawling and tugging at her rope. Papa shakes his head. "Selma, you will take your *skinfeld*," he says, referring to the warm buffalo robe, "and sleep with the boys in the loft." Mama smiles at me, but Jens and Carl pinch up their faces.

I know we will get no sleep tonight.

By morning the storm has passed and the calf has arrived. Licked dry and with a belly full of milk, he unsteadily explores the house. Nellie is back in the pole shed, and Jens and I have cleaned up the mess.

Mama says the calf can stay in the house for a day or two, "until he's learned to drink milk from a pail."

This delights the boys, but Nellie isn't happy. For

the next few days, she makes a racket calling to her calf to come out of the house.

"You should be grateful, old girl. Your calf is alive," Mama exclaims as we watch Nellie from the window.

We make *pot ost* from Nellie's milk. I help Mama boil the colostrum in a large double kettle until it is thick like custard. What a treat it is sprinkled with sugar and cinnamon and extra cream poured over the top!

🎄🎄🎄

Mama brushes my hair before I leave for school with Jens. I sit very still, looking into the oblong mirror on top of the bureau. Her heart-shaped face is peaceful today. She moves the brush through my hair, untangling the long strands. My hair leaps out from my head like sparks from a golden sun ball. It reminds me of our cat Ilsa on a parched August day when the old rooster flew out from behind the house and took her by surprise. The orange hairs on the back of her neck stood up just like mine are right now.

I tell Mama and she laughs out loud. It is the first time she has laughed like that, I think, since dear Lisbet left us last summer.

Mama braids my hair, wrapping it in a circle and pinning it in the back of my head while Jens hollers from the yard to "hurry up!" I know he hates walking to school with his big sister every day. Since he's turned eight, he thinks he can walk by himself.

I hurry to catch up with Jens. He is tall for his age and can run like a deer when he chooses. Along the road, deep furrows made by bobsleighs make our walking difficult. The encrusted snow will not melt until warmer spring winds soften the hard earth into mud. I step carefully, trying to keep my high-buttoned shoes from getting soaked through. I am hoping Fru Bergen will let me sit on a bench to dry out close to the long stove in the front of the room.

Papa said last week that I am getting too old for school...that I will have to stay at home and help Mama when the new baby comes. I will miss learning the new language that is still foreign to my tongue.

🌲🌲🌲

The flame flickers inside the glass globe of the kerosene lamp on the table next to Mama. She rocks in the sturdy oak rocker that her mother sent with her from "the Old Country." The darning needle in her fingers goes in and out of Carl's sock as if it has a mind of its own, so many times has she done this same mending—on Papa's socks, Jens', and Carl's. Shadows from her busy hands dance in rhythm against the rough, plastered wall. The rocker creaks.

I am hoping she will play something on the piano like she used to in the evenings. A lively tune would be fun, then a soft one.

I finish washing the dinner dishes in the kitchen washstand. Our cat Ilsa lies beneath the wood stove's arching belly, enjoying its warmth. Papa has gone out to milk the cows and bed down the horses. Jens is supposed to help him with the milking but he lags behind, playing some silly game with Carl.

When I remind Jens of his evening chores, he and Carl break out in loud voices. They duel with their lath swords, swinging the narrow wood strips at each other. Ilsa jumps up, bumping her head against the bottom of the stove, and scoots back against the wall.

"Boys! Not in the house," Mama scolds. She starts to get up, then with a sharp cry, hunches forward, her hands grabbing her belly. The mending falls to the floor.

We all stare at her. The boys stand with their make-believe swords held in mid-air.

"Jens," Mama says when she gets her breath. "Go get your *pater*. It is the baby."

Jens drops his sword and runs out the front door. Something mean twists inside me. I feel fear for Mama and this baby that wants to come too soon.

I run over to her. She has stopped rocking and looks at me through pain-dimmed dark eyes.

"Selma," she says, "fill the big kettle with vater.... Put it on the stove."

Young Carl starts to cry and I pull him close to me. I know he is remembering our Lisbet. I tell him everything will be fine.

Papa and Jens burst through the door. I send Jens to the well for more water and I throw more wood in the stove. Papa helps Mama onto their straw bed.

Her face is wet with feverish sweat. We loosen her clothing. I pat her face with a corner of the bed sheet. She stares up at Papa. "We must get Kristina Pederson—she will help when the time comes."

My father starts to go out of the room, but she

grasps his hand. "Lars, don't leave me. I must not lose this baby!" Her head turns on the pillow and her gaze falls on me. Papa looks from Mama to me.

"I will go," I hear myself say, although I have no idea how I alone will get to the Pedersons on the opposite side of the big lake.

Papa heaves a long sigh. I can see it is a hard decision for him to make. "Selma," he says finally, "I will hitch up the horses. Do you think you can do this for your mater?"

"I have taken the horses and wagon before, Papa."

Papa nods. From beneath thick eyebrows, his blue eyes reassure me. Then he leaves the room and goes outside, a chill gust invading from under the closing door.

Carl comes running up to the bed and leans over Mama. "Is the baby coming?" His small pinched face looks so concerned.

"*Ja*...soon." She strokes his bent head and draws him closer to her breast.

I stand at the only window in the room, staring out into the dark night. A dim, red light glows from the lantern as Papa hitches the horses to our old wagon. I shiver, thinking that I have only driven the horses once before, last summer to the fields to take Papa and the hired man their lunch. But I am older now, almost twelve, and I must be strong.

I make Mama as comfortable as possible then throw a second woolen shawl around me. Her pains are coming closer now and she holds onto herself. She takes my hand, saying, "You are my brave girl."

I lean over and kiss her warm forehead. Papa is calling and I race out the front door.

He helps me up onto the wagon seat. I look down at the horses, stomping in the cold night air, probably unhappy because they were taken away from the more comfortable pole shed. Their broad backs ripple beneath the lantern's light as Papa hands me the reins. I swallow hard.

Wrapping a heavy *skinfeld* around me, he says, "Don't worry, Selma girl. I would send Jens with you, but then there would be no room for Mrs. Pederson on the way back."

Papa steps away and sets the lantern on the ground. "The horses know the road. Just turn right after the three big pine."

I nod, looking straight ahead.

"God speed," Papa says to me and gives the big fellow on the right a bold smack on his giant rump. "Go boys!"

Then off we fly. The sound of clacking hooves on the frozen earth rings in my ears, makes my heart pound. The northern wind stings my cheeks. We hit the rutted road and I bounce up and down on the seat like a small frog crossing a pond.

Shivering, I manage to pull my shawl up tighter around my head while still grasping the reins tightly. The thought of the baby coming scares me but makes me more determined. I lean forward into the sharp wind, become one with the galloping team and the racing wagon wheels. The constant bobbing of the horses heads, barely outlined in the half moon's light, lulls me into a momentary timelessness.

Suddenly it is last summer. In the yellow field ahead I see the men with their swinging scythes. They toss up clusters of wild strawberries as they near the meadow. Gleefully, we children hurry to fill our buckets with the sweet fruit. We find more in the fragrant grass along the meadow's edge.

"Mama will make *pannkakas!*" Jens declares. Little Lisbet stuffs a handful of the red berries into her mouth, and then another. I try to make her stop, but she runs over to Carl. They grin at me, their cheeks full.

Then we are all riding on a load of wheat sheaves stacked in the wagon. Everyone is jumping up and down, laughing. At two and-a-half years, Lisbet, with carrot curls tumbling down her back, can jump almost as high as her older brother Carl.

The wagon hits a bump and lurches to the side. Lisbet falls. So quickly we cannot catch her. The creaking wagon wheel rolls forward over her.

"Lisbet!" I scream.

We are not far from home. Papa carries her all the way, her still, sweet face cradled against his chest. Blood streaks from her neck. Like crimson ribbons, it weaves through her hair. The boys choke back their sobs. My tears are a scalding river. We know she is gone.

Lisbet is laid to rest beyond the wild plum trees in our small family cemetery. *My sister, my heart.*

Now I squeeze my eyes shut and swallow over the ache in my throat. "Please let this baby wait," I pray out loud. "Please let this baby wait."

The trees become thicker, more clustered, as I near

the end of the lake. Taller and taller they grow on either side of the rutted road. Coal-black witches with gnarled fingers swiping at me from beneath their thorny, flapping robes. Jens says witches lurk in the woods, waiting for children. But Mama says there are angels in the woods. Some are always with us. Even with our Lisbet when she died.

I hope some angels are with me now, and that these horses get me to the Pedersons on faster legs.

We come to a fork in the road where the three big pine loom. I turn the team off to the right. After about half a mile, I see flickering candle light from the windows of the Pedersons' log house. A cry of relief escapes me. Reining in the puffing animals, I jump down from the wagon and stumble to the front door.

"Selma!" Kristina Pederson's round, cheery face greets me on the threshold before I can knock. "Come in from this cold night. How is your mama?" Three little girls cling to her skirts, peeking out at me. Hans, her husband, stands further into the room with their son Olaf. The whole family gathers around me by the fireplace.

"Mama is having the baby!" I splutter out. "She needs you as soon as you can come, Mrs. Pederson."

"*Ja, ja.*" Mrs. Pederson calls the eldest girl to fetch her shawls. "And you must be frozen!" She brings me a mug of steaming coffee with lots of cream and sugar in it. I sip the coffee gratefully but turn away a plate of scones. Hunger does not fill my mind—only thoughts of the baby.

In a short time, we are back on the dark road. Kristina Pederson has packed a few things in a bag for

Mama. She has delivered babies all over our county, and always knows what to do if any trouble arises. She knows these things from talking to the horse doctor who travels through our county twice a year.

I see what Papa meant when he said there would be no room for Jens on the way back. Kristina's wide rump takes up more than half the seat! With the wind nipping at us, though, I am glad for her company and her warmth. I settle back on the seat, relieved that Kristina Pederson is taking the reins.

The first thing I see as we gallop up to the house is Carl's face pressed against the front room window. He is barely tall enough to look out. When he sees us, he begins to hop up and down.

Papa bolts outside and helps Kristina and I climb down from the wagon. "It is good that you could come, Kristina. Sigrie needs you now."

We hear Mama cry out and we hurry in the front door. Papa and Kristina rush to her. Carl wraps himself around me, burying his face in the folds of my skirt.

"Come now, Carl. You must be brave," I say. We climb up into the loft with Jens, sit on the bed and wait. The crackling flames in the fireplace send sparks onto the stone hearth. I try not to think about how painful it must be to give birth.

The grandfather clock chimes at the half hour.

It is not long before we hear a spanking sound, and the new baby wails. The three of us look at each other. The boys' eyes are wide with wonder and excitement.

"Do you think it is a boy or a girl?" Jens says to me. I shake my head, asking myself the same thing.

With great expectation, we stare at the bedroom door below us.

Finally the door opens and out walks Papa holding a small bundle. We scramble down the ladder, almost falling on top of each other. Jens and I peer into a berry-red face that is opening into a serious yawn.

Carl tries to climb up Papa's leg. "Let me see!"

"Here, young fella." Papa bends down, holding the squirming baby under Carl's nose. "Welcome your new baby sister."

It is a happy night. Mama says to fetch the cider jug from the pantry shelf, and I do. Standing around the bed, we all celebrate with a toast to the new girl, "Marie Lisbet."

In the morning, after Papa returns from taking Kristina Pederson home, he goes into the bedroom leaving the door ajar. I look in and see him gaze down at the sleeping baby in her crib, then walk over and take Mama's brush from the dresser. He sits on the bed next to Mama as she lies back on the feather pillows. Her face is so pale, almost as pale as the bed sheet. She looks up at Papa as he takes her long brown hair in his hand and brushes it. Very gently, curling it around his fingertips.

When I see him do this, my heart brims full.

At the front window, I look out into the yard. The boys have finished their chores and are playing Fox and Geese beneath softly falling snow.

Christmas will soon be here.

Lucia Day falls on December 13, a day when our family pays homage to Santa Lucia who in olden times brought light to the long gray Scandinavian winters. The day before, Mama will bake *lussekatter*, fluffy butter buns, tinted golden with saffron.

At church, I will join other girls dressed as Saint Lucia in long white robes and crowns on our heads decorated with lingonberry sprigs. We will carry white candles, lending our voices to the holy celebration. The glazed buns, cookies, and *rulltarta*, sponge cakes spread with homemade jam, will be shared with family and neighbors.

Carl and Jens can't wait for Father Christmas to bring them presents.

Best of all will be the evenings when we sing *God Jul* songs from "the Old Country." I will hold little Marie Lisbet on my lap while I rock her in Grandma's rocking chair. Wearing her best red woolen dress, Mama will sit down at the piano in the far corner beneath the glowing lamp light. She will look over at Papa and smile when she first touches the keys. They will feel cool on her fingertips. Her chin will lift and her dark eyes will close. And then she will play.

The End

Women Writing the West
LAURA Contest
Finalist - 2009
(Original version)

SNOW ANGELS OF SAN MARCIAL

The bus for Socorro rumbles off the gravel onto the highway. Angelina's mother waves from a foggy window, a small brown face framed in a red woolen scarf. Another long day ahead at the pottery plant and another long ride home at dusk await her.

Angelina shivers in the chill of a December morning. Every day during her holiday break from school, she has accompanied her mother to the bus stop. The least she can do. This morning before they left the house, she gave her own gloves to her mother so at least her hands would be comforted before the wet pottery clay could take its daily toll.

Gathering her worn jacket around her, Angelina starts back down the half-mile walk home, her thoughts filled with the misery of the past year. If only her father hadn't been laid off from the factory the previous winter. He'd fallen into a depression from which he could not escape. Sitting on the lumpy sofa and staring out at the arid desert landscape, drinking at the town bar, wandering about the village was the sad and useless way he'd filled his time. Until his kidneys failed. Stranded in San Marcial with no car and no health insurance, he couldn't get the right treatment. Her brothers, Juan and Miguel, found him one afternoon in the alley behind the bar, lying amongst the wine bottles and old newspapers. Asleep forever.

Without much ceremony, they'd buried him in the village cemetery. A visiting priest had given the last sacraments as they laid him to rest near the ancient saguaros he loved. Angelina and her mother had scattered desert flowers across a pine coffin.

This Christmas would be bleak. No Christmas tree. "It would not show respect for your father," her mother had said just the other day. "Too much celebration is not a good thing."

And, so it was. Past due bills poured in steadily. She'd watched her mother's face grow tired, old at thirty-seven. No new clothes this year, no extras, no money.

Angelina approaches the old Plymouth propped on cinder blocks, rotting in the yard beside the house. Faded brown with a rusted green side door, the car hunkers against the New Mexico desert wind like a dead bird, its life blood sucked away.

Memories of childhood suddenly fill Angelina's head, of summer excursions to San Antonio and merry fiestas along the banks of the Rio Grande. Then, riding in the shiny new car, the family had felt a sense of pride. Her mother, perched in the front seat, a vibrant flower in her hair, would look over at her father and laugh at his many jokes. The back seat cushion had felt as soft as a baby chick against Angelina's bare legs.

As she enters the one-story adobe, the voices of Miguel and Juan greet her. They are seated at the kitchen table talking over coffee and tortillas. Miguel works part-time at the one gas station in town. He likes the extra money the job provides but grumbles when he must give half of it to Mama to pay the bills.

"I think I'll quit school and go find a really good job in San Antone, or maybe Albuquerque," Miguel brags to his 13-year-old brother.

"Don't talk like that around Mama," Angelina says, shrugging off her jacket. "You know she wants you to graduate."

"No big deal. She and the old man never did."

"You show no respect, Miguel." Anger sticks like a burr in her throat. "You know they would have if they weren't so poor. They had to go work in the corn fields when they were younger than Juan."

Cocky Miguel makes a face, grabs his faded denim jacket from the wall hook near the front door and leaves for work, banging the door behind him.

Frustrated, Angelina pulls Juan out of his chair— not so easy any more since he is only a year younger and already taller than her—and persuades him to make his bed and take out the trash. She worries that Juan, who always copies his older brother, will follow "crazy Miguel" if he quits high school early. Then where would they be? The thought of both brothers gone, leaving Angelina and her mother to survive alone, overwhelms her.

After adding water to the large pot of beans simmering on the ancient stove, she replaces the lid, combs her long brown hair, puts on her jacket and scarf, and leaves the house. Her destination is the little Catholic church on the other side of the village, a place to find some peace. She walks hurriedly, looking straight ahead, past the plaza fountain, past the lone pinon pine at the side of the plaza, past the corner bar, and past the Shop and Go.

Entering the church, Angelina kneels and makes the sign of the cross, then sits in a front pew. She folds her hands together, cold fingers interlacing. All is quiet in the small sanctuary; she is alone. Father Garcia will preside over mass on Christmas Eve. He visits on holy days only since the parish is too poor to have a full-time priest.

A nativity of carved and painted wooden *santos* has been set up before the plain altar. Angelina gazes into the face of the tiny Christ child as she prays. The vision of her mother's hands, raw and worn, come to her. If only she had the money to buy her mother a pair of warm gloves. Are there tears in the Christ child's eyes? Quickly, she brushes away tears from her own.

Later, as she leaves the church and goes down the front walk to the road, an idea for her mother's Christmas gift comes to her.

The next evening at the Shop and Go, Angelina and her mother buy groceries to last through the holiday weekend. They select several big cans of corn and whole tomatoes, a large bag of flour, ground beef, some onions and chili peppers.

"Is this all, Carlotta?" Lupe Romero, the store manager, asks. "Why not get one of those fat turkeys over there in the freezer?"

Angelina's mother shakes her head. "No, we can't. The bills have to be paid first."

Lupe clucks her tongue. "*Dios mio!* That husband of yours—drinking away his life."

Angelina looks sharply at the large woman who reminds her of a burrowing armadillo with her long snout of a nose. She should remember her own good-for-nothing husband who ran off with a neighbor woman to Alamogordo last year.

Carlotta sniffs into a tissue. "If only we still had the car."

"*Caramba!* If I had a car, I would drive to Santa Fe and buy me some fine dresses and a big fancy Navajo rug." Lupe's small armadillo eyes dart from side to side. "Maybe some real silver jewelry."

Carlotta's dark features grow curious. "Silver jewelry? Where would you wear it?"

With a wave of a large hand, Lupe turns to a customer coming in the front door. "Don't worry, I would wear it."

The following morning, after Angelina walks her mother to the bus, she pays a visit to Lupe at the Shop and Go. She hates to ask this woman for anything, but she is her mother's friend.

"Lupe," she starts hesitatingly. "Since I don't have the money to buy Mama some new gloves, I have another idea. Could I get some paper bags from you to make *farolitos* to set outside the church before mass on Christmas Eve? And candles…those small white candles." Angelina pauses to take a breath. "I'll pay you after I babysit for the Gonzales family."

Lupe agrees. She is a nice armadillo lady, after all.

But when Angelina mentions to Miguel that she needs sand for the *farolitos*, he becomes haughty. "That's a dumb idea, baby sister. Where would I find any sand?" And he saunters away.

"Miguel!" Her fists clench at her sides. *How I would like to punch in your cocky face!* a voice inside her shouts.

Later, however, on the front stoop, she discovers two large tin cans filled with sand. She grins in surprise. What a sly brother, that Miguel.

All the following afternoon Angelina works on her surprise. She carries the large cans of sand down the main street of the village, past the plaza. At the corner bar, she sees Pepe Loco, the town drunk, emerge into the cold, blustery air. Wearing a shabby parka, he weaves in Angelina's direction, but she rushes by, ignoring him. She sets the cans in front of the church and goes back through town to the Shop and Go where she finds Lupe filling the shelves with Wonder bread and packages of pinto beans. "You have the candles we talked about, and the paper bags…?"

Lupe grunts, tossing the last package of pinto beans onto a lower shelf. "*Si, muchacha,* I have them."

"*Gracias,* Lupe. My next babysitting job, I will pay you."

Armed with the precious candles and paper bags, twenty of them, Angelina returns to the church. Carefully setting the slim grocery bags a few feet apart, she pours the sand into each bag thinking, "*Little farolitos, you will make such a beautiful Christmas gift.*" A single candle she anchors at the bottom of every bag. Finally, standing back, she views her work. A promenade of lantern bags on each side of the walk marches from the church door out to the road. Their light will gently flicker tomorrow on Christmas Eve, a glowing entrance to the Christ child's birthday celebration.

On the way home, Angelina braces against the cutting wind, hugging her thin jacket around her chest. Are those tiny snowflakes that sting her forehead and cheeks? The clouded sky churns above her as she reaches her barren yard and scurries to the front door. The threat of snow lurks ever closer. But, here in San Marcial it rarely snows, she reassures herself.

Just before nightfall, Carlotta drags into the house, her face red-raw from the cold. Angelina heats up the black bean soup on the stove and takes a loaf of Indian bread out of the oven for their supper.

Later, Juan helps her clear the table while outside the sleet continues its freezing descent and a relentless wind rattles the windows.

On Christmas Eve morning, after praying to the statue of the Blessed Virgin in the corner of the front room, Carlotta fixes breakfast. As soon as Angelina has finished eating, she pulls on Juan's coat and her old wool hat, tells her mother that she is going to church, and trudges outside. Overnight the wet sleet has become a foot of snow.

A feeling of dread accompanies every step as Angelina hurries through the quiet village. Her worst fear is realized as she approaches the entrance to the church and finds the half-buried *farolitos*. The bags are wet and town; many have blown over. Some of the candles are lost in the snow, and others have snapped in half from the cold.

All my work ruined! Mama's Christmas gift is lost! Sobs overtake her. Heartbroken, Angelina gathers up as many of the bags as she can find before turning back towards home.

Midway through town, she bumps into her brothers as she stumbles along, staring downward at the snow. "Something terrible has happened." Angelina cries out her sad story to them.

Miguel awkwardly pats her on the shoulder. Juan takes the sodden *farolitos* and says, "That is too bad. But don't worry."

Before Angelina reaches home, she stops and dabs her swollen eyelids with snow. *Mustn't let Mama know about this...mustn't make her Christmas any worse.*

The rest of the day Angelina remains withdrawn, unable to put on a cheerful face. When Carlotta asks her if she doesn't feel well, Angelina only shakes her head and looks away, afraid the tears will spill over once again.

Finally, Christmas Eve arrives. The family dresses in their best clothes to go to Christmas Mass. Angelina brushes her mother's hair and arranges it in a sleek bun at her nape. A small gesture but at least it is something to show her love, and lift her sad heart.

They walk through the darkly quiet village, joined by Lupe and other members of their congregation.

Father Garcia, a tall and gracious man, performs the mass while candle votives glimmer with light at the altar. The sanctuary is crowded on this night, the closeness of reverent bodies spreading warmth throughout . Incense leaves its perfumed scent in the air. From the corner of her eye, Angelina sees Miguel and Juan rise silently from the end of the pew and leave the church. Where could they be going? She feels a sense of shame. Have they no respect?

Our father should be here to give them a good shaking!

Church bells chime as the worshippers emerge into newly fallen snow. Angelina breathes in the crisp air and gazes up into the night sky, almost expecting to see that special star. Carlotta grabs her coat sleeve, her round face filled with wonder. *"Dios mio!* Look at the lights."

Angelina rushes to the plaza with her mother and Lupe, and the others. The small pinon tree sparkles with lights of all colors. In the center of the plaza, the little fountain glows, encircled with miniature white lights.

"Like the Virgin's crown," Carlotta cries, staring at the fountain.

Miguel and Juan appear, grinning in fraternal conspiracy. "We did it," they say almost in unison.

"But where did you get them?" Angelina can't believe them.

Miguel's black eyes dance. "Lupe found a bunch of lights in her storeroom at the Shop and Go."

"Oh, Lupe." Angelina squeezes the large woman's arm.

"We did it for everyone—but mostly for Angelina—since the snow ruined her *farolitos*," Juan says in his soft spoken way.

Angelina hugs her younger brother and smiles at Miguel. "You've given my gift to Mama. Thank you both."

Miguel pulls a tambourine from behind his back. "Now we must dance to celebrate this special night." His tall, lanky frame spins and whirls as he starts a circle dance around the plaza fountain. All follow, merrily jumping up and down, swirling round and round. The women, making clucking sounds, raise their arms to the night sky. Tiny snowflakes descend upon them.

"*Feliz Navidad, Feliz Navidad!*" someone sings out. Into the circle sways the familiar chunky figure of Pepe Loco.

Miguel gives the tattered man a shove. "Go away, you drunk."

"Miguel! Where is your Christmas spirit?" Carlotta reprimands.

Too late. Pepe totters and falls backwards in the snow. The villagers stop their dancing. Juan goes forward to help him up. But Pepe lies contented, staring up at the falling flakes. He giggles then begins flapping his arms at his sides.

Lupe laughs out loud. "He thinks he's a bird."

"No! He's making a snow angel," Angelina insists. A flopping sound next to her and young Juan falls onto his back, swishing his arms and legs, making his own angel.

One by one, every member of the circle falls backward into the snow. Laughter and swishing sounds ascend from the plaza of San Marcial as two dozen villagers for a moment become winged snow angels.

Nearby Angelina sees her mother, like a child, catch a snowflake on her tongue. Carlotta looks over at her, her dark eyes full of light. *"Feliz Navidad, mi hija."*

"Merry Christmas, Mama."

Angelina gazes up into the swirling white. Snow drops fringe her eyelashes, settle on her nose. She feels cold and warm at the same time. From the corner of her vision, the lights from the pinon tree twinkle like all the stars in heaven.

The End

ByLine Magazine
Christmas Fiction Contest
First place, 1998

Leslee Breene

CARPENTER'S CRIB

Lauren Goforth closed the car door and settled Skip into his stroller. His chubby fingers grabbed for her loose hair and caught a fistful. "You're cute, tadpole." She smiled, freeing herself from his grasp. "That's what your daddy calls you." Tears pricked her eyelids. *"Called you,"* she corrected herself.

Her lips pressed together tightly as she looked into The Carpentry Shop window. *Your daddy's gone and he's never coming back.*

It had been nine months since Gary's telephone company supervisor called her at the office with the terrible news. Gary had touched a live wire and fallen fifty feet to his death. He'd left her with a special gift: their one-month-old son.

Skip and her receptionist job at the real estate office had become her only lifelines to sanity.

Some days, Lauren still couldn't believe Gary wasn't in the next room or lying next to her when she awoke. They'd planned to build their dream home right here in this small mountain community.

"No big city life for my kids," Gary had said when they packed their belongings and headed out of Denver just a year ago. "We'll move up to where the air is clear and you can hear yourself think."

On the outskirts of town, they rented a small but comfortable house. "Just down the road from all those aspen. That's where we'll buy some land and build our place," Gary had announced with infectious enthusiasm. And hugged her hard after he said it.

A bell on the top of the screen door jangled as Lauren pushed the stroller inside the shop. The smell of linseed oil and furniture stain greeted her. Various pieces of furniture filled the small interior.

The owner of the shop, an auburn-haired man of about thirty, came out of the back room wiping his hands on his faded jeans. Flecks of sawdust clung to his shirt and a sprinkling of freckles paraded across his face. She'd seen him several times at Skip's daycare with his daughter. A spark of recognition brightened his gaze. "Something I can do for you today?"

"Yes," she answered. "Can you make a crib for me?"

"A crib. For you?" Crinkly lines spread outward from the sides of his hazel-green eyes.

"For him," she answered, flustered, glancing down at Skip. "To replace the small one that he has now. A sturdy bed that he can grow into—one that has strong sides—so I won't worry about him falling out."

"Sure, I can do that." He winked at Skip, and the baby smiled up at him. "It'll take about six to eight weeks. My work load is kinda backed up right now."

"That's okay. I can wait." They agreed on a price and she made a down payment. She noticed his hands were large and well-formed, hands that worked wood into designs to fit his customer's dreams.

Driving back home, she thought about what the new crib would look like and the freckles on the carpenter's face. A ripple of guilt tensed her hands on the steering wheel. *It's only been nine months. I still feel like a married woman.*

When Lauren stopped to pick up Skip at his babysitter's after work a few days later, she nearly bumped into the carpenter coming down the front steps. A little red-haired girl about four held his hand. Lauren remembered seeing her among the other children.

"I've started on the crib," he said as they stood on the narrow walk. "By the way, I'm Red Benson and this is my daughter Sherri."

Sherri drew closer to him and said, "Hi." Hazel eyes and freckles on her cheeks, Lauren noted. Just like her daddy.

Hanna Hamilton, the daycare owner, stood balancing a wiggly Skip while talking on her cell phone as Lauren entered one late afternoon of the following week. "Yes, I can keep her here until you can make it." Hanna glanced over her wire-frame glasses at Sherri Benson who lingered by the front window, a dubious expression on her small face.

Lauren guessed that Hannah was talking to Red. All

the rest of the children had been picked up by their parents. Where was Sherri's mom?

"Your daddy has to finish a table for a customer," Hanna explained to the little girl, "and then he'll—"

"I can drop Sherri at the shop," Lauren offered. "It's on my way home."

Sherri's freckled cheeks lifted.

"Lauren will bring Sherri home shortly," Hanna announced and ended the call. She gave Skip over to Lauren. He squealed happily when she took him, warming her heart.

"I saw you talkin' to that handsome Red Benson the other day," Hanna said, lowering her voice. "I hope you don't mind, but when he was admirin' the baby, I told him you were a widow."

Before Lauren could respond, Hanna confided, "He's a widower, you know. He lost his wife in a car accident. Kept pretty much to himself ever since."

"What a shame." A car accident. And he was a widower. What a coincidence.

🌲🌲🌲

"Hey, thanks," Red said when Lauren ushered Sherri into the woodworking shop.

Strangely Lauren's neck and face warmed beneath his glance. "I was glad to help out. Your daughter has a great vocabulary."

"She's a talker." Red looked at her with a twinkle in his eyes. "Well, your good deed deserves a payback. I'm going horseback riding this Saturday afternoon. You want to go?"

"Sure. That would be fun," she heard herself say and, in a daze, pivoted and almost tripped on the threshold as she left.

Once outside, her hands started to shake. *What have I done? I haven't been on a date since before Gary. And I haven't been on a horse since I was ten years old! I'll have to call him as soon as I get home and say that I've made other plans.*

But by the time she drove home, she didn't have the nerve to call Red and back out. It would only hurt his feelings—and she wanted to stay on good terms until he finished the crib.

🌲🌲🌲

Outside of town, two horses waited at the Trail's End hitching post, switching their tails against the flies. The taller one was a mellow tan with white stockings. The shorter one, a pinto, flicked her ears when they approached.

Mischievous elves tied knots in Lauren's stomach as she and Red walked toward the animals. *Why did I agree to this?*

Red sauntered up to the tan horse and stroked his thick mane. "Say hello to Sarge, my riding buddy." Sarge nuzzled Red's palm and found a sugar cube. "Glad to see me, boy?"

She admired his easy way with the horse. Any man who got along so well with horses must have good character.

"That's your little filly." Red went over to the other horse and gave her a sugar cube. "This is June Bug."

Lauren smothered a chuckle. "June Bug?"

"She's gentle, and just your size." Red angled his head in her direction. "C'mon over here and I'll help you up."

Lauren minced over to the horse, wishing her nearly-new boots would stop pinching her toes. Red's hand on her arm felt rough in a reassuring way, and strong. After she'd made two attempts to throw her leg over the saddle, he gave her bottom a boost.

Her face burning with embarrassment, she landed in the saddle.

Her rear had barely touched leather when Red drawled, "Let's ride." Off they went beneath clusters of aspen, their leaves shimmering golden in the morning sun.

After what seemed like an endless half hour of trotting, they came to a narrow creek and Sarge crossed easily. But June Bug balked.

"Just give her rein," Red called. "Dig in your heels!"

Lauren dug in her heels. June Bug skittered sideways. "Don't think she wants to cross."

Red watched from the other side, his cowboy hat sloped half-way down over his eyes. "I thought she'd crossed this creek before. Well, try it again."

She did. June Bug backed away. Then, something long and striped slithered through the stubbled grass in front of them. June Bug whinnied and reared onto her hind legs. Lauren shrieked.

"Hang on!"

Nerves jangled, hands perspiring, she grasped the reins and choked out, "Whoa, girl. Whoa, girl."

Sarge kicked up walls of water as Red rode him

back to meet her on the other bank. "You okay?"

She nodded shakily. "I saw a snake!"

He reached over and took June Bug's reins from her before starting across the creek. "Probably just a garter snake," he said with a lopsided grin. "It must have spooked her."

Lauren cringed. "Oh…just a garter snake."

After the ride, they went for hamburgers at the Sundown Café in town. Red was easy to talk to, and the conversation centered on Sherri and Skip. But when Red started telling her about his wife, Lauren's breath seemed trapped in her chest.

"Her car skidded off an icy mountain road over a year ago on the way home from her parents," he said quietly. "I told Sherri her mom went to heaven and wasn't coming back. It was the hardest thing I ever had to do."

A familiar lump formed in Lauren's throat. She couldn't talk about Gary. Not to Red. Not yet. Maybe not ever.

As they walked to his pickup, Red slipped his fingers through hers. She couldn't decide if she liked the touch of his warm hand holding hers. She eased hers away when he opened the passenger side door.

"I guess horseback riding wasn't such a good idea for a first date," he said good-naturedly as they stepped up onto her small front porch. "Next time, you choose."

She couldn't stop the little smile that lifted the corners of her mouth. "Okay."

He moved closer, catching her off guard, and

placed his hand on her shoulder. His warm lips pressed against one side of her mouth, left her short of breath and tingling all over. It was a gentle kiss that begged for another. But she pulled back.

It didn't feel right. It was too soon. A casual date was all she'd expected.

She avoided his eyes which she knew were full of questioning. "I have to go in." Blood thundering at her temples, she opened the screen door, thanked him and ducked inside.

In the following weeks, mountain property sales and rentals, which had been slow, began to pick up and Lauren worked late at the real estate office. The last leaves of autumn blew through the streets on chill winds. She saw Red only once or twice when she picked up Skip after work. He would usually be helping Sherri into his pickup or driving away in a swirl of dust. With a quick wave, he would disappear down the road. When she waved back, a strange little ache tugged at her heart.

🌲🌲🌲

A few days before Thanksgiving, she stood at the screen door, holding the baby as Red unloaded the crib from his truck. Powerful muscles beneath his flannel shirt rippled across his back in the sunlight.

"Your big boy crib is here!" she declared to Skip, her heartbeat fluttering against her rib cage.

Red set the bed in the corner of Skip's room. It was just the right height and smelled of fresh wood stain.

"I love it," she said simply. She went to the crib and

trailed her fingers over its smooth surface. "I love the color—like dark honey."

"It matches the color of your hair," he said, then cleared his throat. "You can lock this side in place so Skip can't fall out."

Red demonstrated how the side rail worked, and their hands touched briefly. His felt callused and strong. Lauren found herself staring straight into those hazel-green eyes and her stomach did a cartwheel. She had to tamp down the urge to hug Red that very minute to thank him for making such a beautiful bed for her son.

"I can make a pot of coffee if you'd like to.... I baked some pumpkin cookies this morning."

He smiled. "Sure." Red played with Skip while she gingerly measured the coffee and placed four large pumpkin cookies on one of her best Blue Danube china plates.

Over steaming mugs, they made small talk and the cookies disappeared. Would he ask her out again? She wouldn't blame him if he didn't.

As Red went to leave, he lingered for a minute at the front door, his broad shoulders filling the doorframe. "Thanks for the coffee. You're a great baker." His quiet gaze held hers, his thoughts unreadable.

"Thank you for the crib. Skip is going to love it."

He reached out and brushed smooth knuckles along her cheek. "Maybe we can try another date, when you're ready."

Beneath his gentle gaze, her face flushed with heat;

her mouth went dry as a hollow husk. Why couldn't she say yes to his offer?

"Don't be afraid to start over, Lauren," he said softly. "I have."

After he left, she chided herself. Wouldn't Gary have wanted her to move on with her life and Skip's...to give her a chance to grow whole again?

The first of the week, Lauren told Hanna about the crib.

Hanna's eyes grew large behind her wire-frame glasses. "Oh, yes. It's all that man could talk about for the last month—how he was workin' on the baby's crib. Just like it was for one of his own."

Lauren's anxious expression must have shown on her face.

"Now, don't get yourself in a stew, dear. You just bring Skip to the Christmas Bazaar this weekend, and please bring a pie for the library fund auction."

Sunday afternoon at the Rock Ridge Library, Lauren set her pie next to others displayed on the long, red-white-and-green draped table. Hers was a candy cane custard pie with a dark chocolate crust, a favorite recipe borrowed from her aunt Dore. She wasn't the best pastry chef, but she was glad to make a contribution to the county library's annual holiday event.

Behind her a familiar female voice crowed, "My triple berry pie won first place at the bazaar last year." Lauren turned and almost bumped into Veryl Crocker, a waitress at the Sundown Café, and Red Benson, looking more handsome than he had a right to in dark western hat, open-necked shirt, and snug-fitting jeans. He glanced good-naturedly at her and back to Veryl who ignored Lauren.

Veryl leaned in close to Red, sliding her peacock-blue fingernails up his arm. "Hope you'll bid on mine, honey."

Lauren turned away, but not quickly enough to miss an unwanted glimpse of the waitress's slim hips in cheek-tight jeans, switching to and fro as she and Red strolled alongside the display tables of varied holiday wares.

Why did a fiery coal form in the center of Lauren's chest and burn up her throat? Why should she even care if Veryl flirted with Red? Or, if he let her?

When the pie bidding began, Lauren hung back behind the elementary school principal, Zada Totter, a middle-aged woman twice her size. She held Skip in her arms, helping him drink fruit juice from a plastic cup.

The rotund pie auctioneer continued along the table until he reached Lauren's pie. Veryl Crocker's celebrated berry pie sat right next to it. Lauren warned herself not to expect much on the results of her entry.

"Who'll start the bidding on this candy cane pie?" the auctioneer prompted the crowd.

"Twenty dollars," her boss, Bill Downs, offered.

Lauren exhaled a sigh of gratitude. At least her pie would go home with someone. She peeked around Zada Totter and saw Red standing tall and sturdy as a ponderosa pine in the front row. *He's probably getting ready to bid on Veryl's masterpiece.*

The auctioneer held up her pie, examining it closely. "The sign says this pie has a dark chocolate crust. Yum."

"I'll give thirty dollars," hollered Joe Cramer, the hardware store manager.

With a flip of her scraggy ponytail, Veryl Crocker sided up to Red. Lauren jerked back causing Skip to spill the remainder of his juice down the front of her dress.

"Fifty dollars!"

Was that Red Benson's voice? Lauren mopped the sticky drink with a tissue while juggling Skip.

"No one's ever bid that much for a pie," Zada declared to a woman standing next to her.

"Fifty dollars.... Do I hear more?" The crowd fell silent.

"Fifty...Fifty dollars. Fifty it is!" The auctioneer lifted up Lauren's pie, holding it like a trophy. "Ms. Lauren Goforth's Christmas pie goes to the gentleman in the front row."

Amidst enthusiastic applause, Red Benson stepped forward and accepted her pie as if it were made of gold.

Lauren froze in place while Skip squirmed to get down out of her arms, eager to crawl across the room. It was definitely time to put him in his stroller and take him home for a nap. To her surprise, Red was making his way through the onlookers, a confident set to his broad shoulders, in her direction. Veryl Crocker scowled after him like an agitated mule.

When he reached Lauren, he stopped and sent her a mischievous wink. "Think you can make me a cup of coffee to go with a piece of your pie?"

She was certain all eyes focused on her. Her face flushed hot and moist as a kitchen sponge. A bead of sweat trickled downward between her breasts. "That could be arranged," she managed, gazing up at him with embarrassed pleasure. "Tomorrow night?"

Red nodded, touched his hat brim, and sauntered away. Lauren's spirits soared. Red would be welcome company during her first Christmas without Gary.

That evening, Lauren bathed and tucked Skip into his crib. Softly she crooned a lullaby to him until his blond lashes drifted down upon round cheeks. As she leaned over to kiss his fragrant tousled head, her hands braced on the side of the crib railing. Strong, smooth-polished wood caressed her fingertips.

She raised up slowly, picturing the capable hands of the craftsman who had built this bed to her specifications, fitted it together to last for years to come, sanded and stained it to a glowing sheen. Her heart swelled, knowing the pride the carpenter had taken in making this piece of furniture with his own hands.

🌲🌲🌲

News about the fire spread fast. Her boss, Bill Downs, was discussing it with one of the real estate agents when Lauren arrived at work the next morning.

"They think it was a short in the wiring—caused the hot water heater to explode last night in the Sundown

Cafe," Bill explained. "Caused major damage there and also burned down that furniture shop next door."

Electric currents buzzed through Lauren's veins. *The Carpentry Shop!*

"My friend owns that place. I've got to see if he's okay," she called to her boss. Grabbing her tote bag, she raced out the front door.

Questions pounded in her head as she drove into the middle of town. Was Red hurt in the fire? Would anything be left of his shop?

She slammed on her brakes at the end of the block, parked the car, and ran down the street. A group of townspeople had gathered in front of the burnt-out buildings. The cafe and the furniture shop were cordoned off. Black soot covered the front of the shop. Pieces of the roof hung in limp tatters, visible through the empty window.

Where was Red? She pushed past some onlookers and entered the shop through the open front door. The odor of burned wood, insulation, and chemicals assaulted her. Inside the gutted interior, she saw him. Crouching down in a corner, he was examining a blackened dining room table. She rushed to his side. "Red, I'm so sorry."

Looking at her with concern, he stood up slowly. "Lauren. You shouldn't be here." His gaze traveled over the burned out shell. "It isn't safe."

"I had to come."

He paced back and forth amid the sooty remains of what used to be his thriving business. "I had such plans for this place. To expand…. Hire an apprentice…." He stopped, raised his hands in a hopeless gesture. "Now this—just before Christmas…."

His devastation wakened a new awareness in her. She looked at Red and realized she had denied her growing feelings for this honorable man. No longer could she cling to the past, when the present compelled her to go forward.

"You can rebuild this shop," she insisted.

He stared at the floor and shook his head. "What about my customers? Their furniture…?"

"Your customers will understand. They'll just have to celebrate Christmas a little late this year."

He grimaced. "Yeah, after the insurance company settles up with me."

Lauren closed the distance between them. She cradled his smudged face in her hands. "We've both lost things and people we've loved. But we can't let it keep us down." Her voice choked with tears, but she continued. "You're strong, Red, I know you can start over. I'm here. I'll help you—if you help me start over, too."

Slowly his arms encircled her, pulling her close.

Lauren gazed up into shadowed hazel eyes. Did she see a ray of hope there? A smile began to spread across Red Benson's face.

He bent his head, his lips lingering very close to hers. Red was going to kiss her, and this time she would let him. When he did, tenderly, his kiss held a promise that filled her empty heart with hope.

From somewhere nearby came a chorus of carolers, the silvery jingle of sleigh bells. In a shaft of light on the edge of darkness, she envisioned a child's crib, tied up with bright red bows, beside a glowing pine-scented Christmas tree.

The End

THE CHRISTMAS GIFT

December 1883

Bright brown eyes in a laughing face captured Miriam's attention. Lips curled upward like a cupid's bow. "You're a handsome young man," she declared above the rumble of train wheels on steel tracks. She held Christopher steady on her lap as he balanced on wobbly legs, trying to look out the window. The world outside of dry winter wheat fields beneath cloudy skies was no doubt a complete mystery to a curious six-month-old baby.

"Wait 'til Aunt Serena sees you," she whispered into the swath of dark wavy hair near Christopher's ear. Not *Aunt* Serena. Soon her older married sister would become Christopher's mother. An immediate rush of excitement filled her. The import of Miriam's journey overtook her senses as it had this morning when she and the baby first boarded the Atchison, Topeka and Santa Fe at Hutchinson. She had been designated by her family to deliver Christopher to her sister in Denver where he would begin his life anew. Three brothers would welcome him as their youngest sibling.

A telegram had arrived, confirming Christopher's acceptance. The Cole family rejoiced at the first uplifting turn of events since the recent passing of their youngest daughter Beth from a virulent siege of influenza. Christopher's father was nowhere to be found, rumor having it that he'd up and run off to live the cowboy life in Texas. Since Mrs. Cole, the matriarch of the family, had passed on five years before, the only option for the child was to find a qualified family member to take him in.

Christmas would take on a most special meaning this year. For Miriam as well. After living all of her twenty-seven years on the farm, except for occasional junkets to visit great aunts and cousins in Topeka, she was venturing for the first time to Denver, a jewel of the western state. The "Queen City of the Plains." Denver promised scenic and social opportunities nonexistent in Kansas.

Instead of viewing miles of wheat fields in all directions, from Denver one viewed endless snow-capped mountain peaks, she had heard. Fine restaurants were plentiful, theatrical productions arrived monthly from the East. Not that she could afford to go to such places. She would just like to see their fancy menus and read about them in the newspapers. Perhaps window shop with her sister to see the latest fashions.

Surveying her traveling dress, a simple forest green wool with high-buttoned collar, Miriam vowed to put her sewing skills to work on a new creation after she arrived in Denver.

Christopher interrupted her thoughts with a lyrical babble then turned his head to gaze across the aisle. Miriam glanced in that direction, noticing a gentleman dressed in black, absorbed in his newspaper. She recalled he'd boarded in Great Bend. Guessing his age to be a few years over thirty, she admired the fit of his long winter coat beneath a clean shaven jaw, full mustache and long sideburns. Most likely he was a rancher traveling to Colorado on business.

From the front of the car came a whoosh of cold air as the conductor entered and slid the door closed behind him. The sight of a revolver jutting out from his hip holster sent a little tingle of apprehension down Miriam's spine.

"We'll be stoppin' for lunch in Dodge City in thirty minutes," he announced as he came up the aisle. "The Harvey House. It ain't much, but the place is clean and the food's pretty good. I'll take your orders now."

A male passenger in the row ahead remarked, "Glad to hear there's somethin' still decent in that roarin' hell town." Gossip along the line warned that Sheriff Bat Masterson couldn't protect the trains from rowdy cowboys intent on shooting out locomotive headlights, or wreaking havoc in rail yards.

After making her lunch order, Miriam tucked her purse farther into the depths of her skirt pocket, hoping that no wayward toughs would cause her or her fellow travelers any trouble.

On the outskirts of Dodge, expansive cattle pens ran parallel to the tracks. Mercifully the din emitted from their bawling occupants was muted in the closed train car. Growing fidgety on Miriam's lap, Christopher banged on the window with a flat pudgy hand. She wrestled him away in hopes of averting his attention to a small wooden horse his grandpa had carved from a pine bough. Instead the baby raised his hands upward, crimping tiny fingers on each side of her head, and pulled handfuls of hair loose from her neatly coiffed bun. Instantly an auburn veil cascaded over her shoulders and onto the front of her dress. A loud giggle burst from his mouth.

"Oh, Christopher!" she gasped. Attempting to hold him with one hand, she pushed a thick wedge of hair behind her left ear. The baby jiggled back and forth on her lap. Clearly, it would take two hands to repair the damage, and keep him from falling.

To her right, a dark blurry figure moved near. "Pardon me, ma'am. May I assist?" a deep male voice asked. She peered through her errant locks, determining the voice belonged to the mustached passenger across the aisle.

A warm flush shot up her neck and into her face. "Oh, I don't—"

Before she could object, strong hands scooped Christopher into sturdy arms. She held her breath sure that the baby would scream in fright of the stranger but was relieved, after sweeping her hair away from her eyes, to see Christopher grinning up into the man's face. A wind-weathered face with serious yet warm hazel eyes. He held the toddler while she tucked and poked strands of long hair back into the bun at the nape of her neck.

"Thank you. That was very kind of you," she said when she'd finished, aware that nearby passengers were observing their conversation.

The gentleman held Christopher a moment longer, as if enjoying the opportunity, then returned him to her. "My pleasure, ma'am. He's an active little fellow." His tall frame folded back into his seat where he resumed reading the newspaper.

Shortly after, the train pulled into its rest stop at Dodge. Across from the platform, two box cars perched on stilts. A large sign on one car read: The Harvey House.

"The first car is the dining room—the next is the kitchen," a blustery-faced male passenger replied to Miriam's inquiry. Thanking the man, she wrapped Christopher's blanket closely around him and deboarded the train. Outside, a riled wind whipped her skirt and prairie dust pricked her nose. With an onset of hunger pangs, she entered the noisy dining car, welcoming the aroma of freshly made coffee. With luck, a stool at the end of the counter was available in the quickly filling car.

A Harvey Girl waitress soon approached wearing a black frock with a crisp white collar and starched white apron. Impressed at the young woman's appearance, Miriam asked, "Do you have fresh milk for the baby?"

"Yes, we have." Her smile was reassuring. "I can warm the milk for him."

"With a little water added, please...."

The waitress nodded. "Would he like a small sugar lump in it?"

Miriam instantly liked this young dark-haired

woman. "Yes, please." Since her sister had passed away, a wet nurse from a neighboring farm had generously offered to nurse Christopher. Over the past few days, Miriam had weaned him onto cow's milk and water.

She glanced down the busy counter and noticed the mustached gentleman from the train, conversing with several other travelers. So far, all of her acquaintances on this winter journey had been courteous and helpful. Yet the thought of traveling the rest of the way to Denver caused a swirl of unease in her empty stomach.

Christopher welcomed his lunch. His plump hands grasped the bottle, accompanied by happy gurgling sounds. Miriam's lunch, a satisfying beef stew, arrived followed by a slice of warm apple pie and coffee.

She marveled at the efficiency and courteous manners of her waitress despite the jostling amid loud patrons in the cramped dining car. This young woman no doubt stood in sharp contrast to the "painted ladies" of the nearby saloons. She'd never encountered a painted lady, but could imagine what they looked like from a few magazine illustrations she'd seen.

Through the passengers' conversation, she'd heard that Harvey Girls received a comfortable weekly salary of $17.50 plus tips, room and board. Not that Miriam would want to reside in raucous Dodge City, but being employed at a Harvey House in another city piqued her interest. She left a ten cent tip for her waitress. Some of the patrons pushed away from the counter without leaving any coins by their plates. That was rude in light of their excellent service.

Sleet and snow on a strong westerly wind pelted the

window as the train pulled out of Dodge. Chilled air inside the car made Miriam glad that their seat was closer to the small wood stove in the rear. But the pungent odor of cigar smoke from the man seated in front of her made her queasy. Fortunately his female traveling companion, presumably his wife, badgered him until he put it out. Pipe smoke she wouldn't have minded but cigar smoke was repugnant.

Oblivious to his surroundings, Christopher finished his bottle and blissfully dozed in her arms. His long dark lashes feathered above full rosy cheeks. The treasure she carried to her sister was beyond worldly measure. Resting her chin on his warm forehead, she closed her eyes.

Screeching train wheels on narrow tracks jolted her from slumber. She blinked and stared outside at a driving snow on either sides of the train. At least four inches had fallen on the ground and the landscape blurred. The whistle bellowed. The train slowed to a jerky stop.

"What was that...?" croaked the woman seated in the row ahead.

Christopher frowned, raising a small fist from beneath his swaddling blanket.

Ushering in a blast of frigid air, the conductor entered the car. "Sorry folks, there's a tree fallen across the track. The crew is working to remove it as quick as they can," he hollered, then brushed past, hurrying into the next car.

Several men seated in the back left to see if they could assist the train crew.

A chorus of moans rippled through the car. Startled

from sleep, Christopher let out a shriek which erupted into a wail. His cherub features contorted, turning as red as a Mexican pepper. When rocking him in her arms didn't assuage the wailing, Miriam rose to her feet and paced the aisle front to back, her eyes averted. Her own face burned with the heat of frustration. This was not an occurrence she'd anticipated.

Christopher wailed on. "That little fellow has a strong pair of lungs," observed the former cigar smoker. Miriam ignored his comment and continued to walk the aisle, hoping to calm Christopher. Which is worse, she thought, a crying baby or obnoxious cigar smoke?

"He can play with my clown," a small blonde girl offered as Miriam came back down the aisle. She held up a clown doll with big painted-on eyes and wide-grinned mouth. Christopher's teary eyes widened when the girl held the clown up to him. Miriam breathed out a long sigh of relief. "Thank you."

She asked the girl's parents if she could come back to her seat and play for awhile. They smiled agreeably. Soon Christopher made a new friend, his usual sunny disposition returning.

Miriam welcomed this small mortal angel on their journey.

When the men returned to the car, the girl went back to sit with her parents, and the train lurched forward, smoke billowing outside the window from the surging engine. From the corner of her eye, Miriam acknowledged the sympathetic smile directed at her from the mustached gentleman on the opposite side of the aisle. She made note that he was almost handsome when he smiled.

Hours later, the train rolled into the Pueblo, Colorado station. Miriam went directly to the ticket counter to purchase her one way ticket to Denver, leaving within the hour. Locating the ladies washroom, she welcomed the opportunity to take care of Christopher's needs, wash out his baby bottle, and refresh herself.

Snow continued to fall, only lighter, as passengers boarded the Denver and Rio Grande train cars. Ahead, she recognized several fellow travelers from the AT&SF boarding a first class car. The tall, black-coated gentleman was among them. His financial means were no doubt more lucrative than hers. The second class car was fairly comfortable with padded seat cushions, although the aisle was as narrow as before. She found a window seat in the rear, close to the warm stove.

The landscape appeared dreary and flat in the approaching dusk, and she tucked an extra folded blanket behind her head. Christopher's head nodded sleepily into the crook of her neck. Soon they both drifted off to the steady rhythm of train wheels on track. When she awoke, the snow had abated. A purple silhouette of mountain range was barely visible to the west.

She shifted the baby in her arms, imagining the advantages he would have growing up with parents and siblings. How best suited her sister Serena and husband Richard would be to guide him along. The things they could provide for him and teach him, things they had experienced raising children of their own.

Life on the farm had its benefits—the satisfaction of being self-sufficient, owning your land. But, her father and brothers were born to the soil, hardworking, sometimes rough-edged. Her father was a no-nonsense man. She tried to recall the last time he'd laughed out loud. And couldn't. A smile was a rare accompaniment to his weathered, set face. He was a godly man, not one given to frivolity. Growing the crops held his undivided attention.

Christopher was not cut from the same cloth. His fine features resembled his mother, his dark eyes always alight with ready humor, his hands plump, but long-fingered. Beth had told Miriam how much she loved his daddy—his spirit, his easy laugh—how her husband could make her laugh. Certainly there was not enough joy in this hard scrabble life. Thinking of Beth and how she had just wanted to make her own life's way, away from the heavy workload on the farm, caused a sudden heartache. Tears rimmed her eyes.

Through the window, she saw a frosting of light snow on the branches of passing tall fir trees. A renewed hope filled her. "Great opportunities await you, Christopher," she whispered into the shell of his ear.

At last, Denver's skyline came into view. Electric lights glimmered from downtown buildings. The Union Station depot loomed ahead. Miriam craned her stiff neck to see more out of the foggy windows after waking from a cramped sleep. Christopher resisted waking despite the surrounding chaos of roused passengers and train whistles from the rail yard.

Inside, she found an available cart and loaded the baby and her belongings into it. Sometime later, after pushing the heavy cart around the cavernous station and not seeing Serena or Richard anywhere near the front entrance, a feeling of unease overtook her. Where were they? Hadn't they checked the train arrival times from Pueblo? She had their home address, but she was sure they didn't have a telephone.

Hating indecision, she wrapped her wool shawl around her head and shoulders and ventured outside to the front walk. The streetlights and sounds of humanity, horse-pulled vehicles and vendors was enticing. Like walking unexpectedly into a circus arena. If only she could enjoy the first-time experience rather than be at a loss as to how she would get to where she wanted to go.

To her right, travelers were lined up along the curb, appearing to solicit carriages for hire. Miriam thought of the small amount of money in her purse. Perhaps she could hire a carriage and share it with other passengers. Midway up the line, she noticed the gentleman who'd assisted her on the train, talking with a driver. She pushed her cart hurriedly up to him. He turned as she approached. "Good evening, sir," she began. "Are you hiring a coach?"

He tipped his western, brimmed hat. "Evening, ma'am. Yes, I've just hired a carriage." He angled his head, looking at her and the baby with polite curiosity. "I'd be happy to have you join me."

She knew her relieved sigh was audible. "Thank you. We're not going far...just up town...to my sister's home." She handed him the written address which he gave to the driver.

"That would be fine, ma'am." He assisted her and the baby into a large enclosed carriage, and the driver put her baggage on top. The cushioned leather seat was the most comfortable she'd ever settled into. The shawl slid to her shoulders as she cradled Christopher in her weary arms.

The gentleman removed his hat and held it in his lap. "I should introduce myself," he said. "I'm Joe Moore."

"I'm Miriam Cole—and this is Christopher, my nephew." She looked down for a moment at the sleeping baby.

"It's my pleasure to meet you both." His eyes held a mysterious twinkle in the reflected street lights.

"I can't imagine what could have happened to my sister and brother-in-law," she rambled on. "They're expecting us. We're here for the first time in Denver…for Christmas."

"No doubt, they'll have a good reason for their delay."

The sound of horse's hooves clopping along the road and the sight of so many foreign buildings seemed as though they were traveling in a magical place. "Do you have family in Denver, Mr. Moore?" The question escaped from her lips before she realized it might not have been any of her business.

He nodded. "I'm visiting my brother's family over the holidays. Seemed like a good time to take some time off from my ranch."

"How nice for you." That he was a ranch owner

impressed her. Her gaze fell to his left hand. He wore no wedding band. She quickly glanced out the window, hoping he hadn't noticed her curiosity.

The carriage rounded the corner onto Lawrence Street, causing her shoulder to momentarily touch his. It was solid, compact. A moment later, the driver reined in the horse in front of a two-story brick building on the corner. "Kruger's Hardware," Joe said, reading the sign above the lighted doorway.

"This must be their store." Miriam peered upward to the second story where lights beckoned behind curtained windows. The driver unloaded her large bag while Joe helped her alight from the carriage. "I can't thank you enough for sharing your conveyance." She reached down into her pocket for her purse. "What do I owe you?"

He smiled and tipped his hat. "Nothing, Miss Cole. It was my pleasure."

At that moment, the front door flew open and a dark-haired woman burst through it. "Miriam, oh, Miriam. I'm so happy to see you!" The overhead light set off the familiar features of Miriam's sister Serena, emphasizing the hollows beneath her eyes. In the two years since she had visited the family farm, she had aged, appearing older than her thirty years. "I'm sorry we couldn't meet you at the station. Richard injured his arm yesterday, and he didn't want me to take the carriage out alone at night."

The two women hugged, Christopher crunched between them. He only frowned beneath his blanket. "It's so good to be here. I knew something was amiss when I couldn't find you at the station."

"Come in, dear," Serena implored, starting to pull her inside. Miriam turned to introduce her kind traveling companion, but he had already hopped aboard the carriage and it was moving away from the boardwalk. Serena picked up Miriam's heavy bag and they entered the store, chattering away like two chickadees. "I've put the boys to bed. They were so disappointed not to see you—and the baby," she said as she led Miriam through the store to a stairway at the rear. "They'll be excited to greet you in the morning."

Miriam followed her. "It will be wonderful to see them again."

Richard stood at the top of the stairs, a stocky blond man, his right arm in a sling. After a brief reunion, they showed Miriam to the spare bedroom at the end of a dimly lit hallway. Furnishings in the small room were spare, but included a baby crib in one corner by the single bed. "The crib was Teddy's," Serena offered, referring to her youngest. "There's soap and fresh water in the basin on the dresser, so you can clean up when you like."

"Thank you. See you in the morning." After Serena closed the door behind her, Miriam tucked the baby into the crib, undressed, and crawled under the bed covers, exhausted from her long day's journey.

A light shining through the sheer curtains and hushed voices wakened her. Three small boys, like stair steps, observed her from the foot of the narrow bed. Two dark, unruly mops of hair and one small tow-head. Freckles and shy grins. "Good morning, Aunt Miriam," their voices chimed together.

She sat up, pushed a lock of hair away from her eyes, and blinked. "Good morning, boys."

"We came to ask you to come to breakfast," said the tallest.

A sudden chirp from the crib and then a wail brought Miriam to her bare feet on the cold hardwood floor. Abruptly her first day in Denver began.

She readied Christopher and brought him downstairs to the kitchen where a hearty breakfast of sausages and eggs cooked on the stove. Miriam's gift of homemade peach jam complemented her sister's hot baking powder biscuits. The nephews' early shyness gave way to competition over getting Christopher's attention.

The Kruger household followed a daily schedule, accomplished by Serena's careful planning, Richard's attention to business details, and a large combined amount of elbow grease.

After the older boys were dashed off to school, Serena opened the store until Richard removed his arm sling several days later and could help her. Miriam took care of Christopher and Teddy, the three-year-old. The women did the grocery shopping and cooked the meals. The boys shared chores in the afternoon.

On Friday, the hired girl arrived early and disappeared into the rear laundry room to do the washing. Church was a family ritual on Sunday. Wearing their best attire, the boys' hair slicked back neatly, their shoes polished, Richard in top hat and long coat, Serena and Miriam in woolen frocks with matching veiled hats, they strolled over to Colfax Avenue and attended the Methodist Church. Afterward, they took a horse-drawn car past Broadway to a favorite German restaurant for their midday dinner.

At day's end, Miriam would retreat to her room with Christopher, her head spinning with new experiences and her body weary from the constant needs of the household. She was growing to love this family, grateful that they were taking her in—accepting Christopher into their lives. The baby was thriving with all the affection showered on him by the boys. However, after a week's stay, she wondered why Serena gave him little notice. She'd hardly held him but once on the morning after their arrival. Admittedly the physical demands upon her sister were many. Richard expected her to be his right arm in running the store, even as his arm healed and he no longer needed the sling.

But was her sister's seeming disinterest in Christopher a normal reaction, considering that she would soon become his mother?

After heating water in the kitchen and bathing Christopher in the little washtub, Miriam would gently pat him dry and apply a bit of talcum. She prided herself in keeping him clean. In a rocking chair in the bedroom, she'd rock him to sleep, his bright brown eyes slowly closing, one plump hand resting on her breast. Whispering a prayer for his divine protection, she would lay him in the crib. On more than one evening, a tear slid silently down her cheek as she gazed at him in the shadowed room. As much as she loved Christopher, how could she ever let him go?

A fortnight before Christmas, Miriam stood in the kitchen next to Serena preparing risen bread dough for the oven. Five large bread pans sat on the counter, greased and floured. "I'll bake Mother's Yule *kuchen* this week," Miriam said while placing the dough into the pans. "Do you have cinnamon?"

Serena wiped beads of perspiration from her forehead, her face pale despite the heated room." Yes. The boys would like that," she replied in a faint voice.

Miriam bent to place the bread pans into the hot oven when Serena suddenly ran from the room to the rear lavatory. What ailed Serena? She'd been noticeably withdrawn for the last several days.

After her sister returned, the women finished cleaning up the kitchen. Soon the yeasty aroma of baking bread filled the room. "There's nothing like the smell of fresh bread," Miriam enthused. "It always makes me hungry."

Serena plopped down on a wooden stool. "I wish I had an appetite. I've been having the morning sickness…."

Taken aback, Miriam stared at her sister. "Morning sickness?"

Serena met her questioning gaze. "I've missed two monthlies…I'm pregnant."

Miriam braced herself against the center butcher block. "Are you sure?"

"This will be my fourth child, Miriam. I know."

Each fell silent, weighing the import of Serena's revelation. "Have you told Richard?"

"No. I'm afraid to." She sighed. "This wasn't in our plans."

A heavy vise crushed Miriam's rib cage. *What will happen to Christopher?*

Serena interrupted her thoughts. "I imagine you're thinking about Christopher. I've been thinking about him too. It's obvious that you love him. Probably more than I ever could."

Tears burned behind Miriam's eyelids. She nodded, fighting back sudden emotion.

"What would you say to taking him as *your* son? Staying on with us and raising him as your own?"

As my own? A tiny flare of exhilaration ignited in her breast. "But, how could I?"

Serena rose from the stool and came to her. "You'd make a devoted mother, Miriam. Beth would be so grateful to you. We would want you to live here, room and board free."

The thought left Miriam speechless.

Serena put her arm around Miriam's shoulder. "The boys already love Christopher like a brother. We would just be—a bigger family."

Joy tinged with confusion overwhelmed her. When she dared look into Serena's eyes, she saw love there…the support she would need to accept this unexpected gift, this life-changing challenge.

In the days that followed, Miriam carried on an intense inner dialogue.

Christopher was the greatest gift she would ever be given. And the greatest responsibility.

Who was she to assume that she could raise a child on her own? Did she have a choice?

Every indication persuaded her that this was what God wanted her to do. How fortunate that she had a family to stand by her.

Midweek she arranged with Serena to take time off to finish her Christmas shopping. On a crisp but sunny morning, she bundled Christopher into Teddy's baby carriage and ventured down Fifteenth Street. Throngs of businessmen, shoppers, and vehicles moved along the walkway and thoroughfare. A buoyant mix of voices, sounds and city smells surrounded her. An aroma of brewed coffee from one shop. A drift of roasting chestnuts from a street vendor.

Her desire to stay in this "Queen City" was palpable. There was no turning back. She would not return to the farm…that part of her life was behind her now.

Attired in her Sunday burgundy frock with ivory lace collar, her mother's pearl drop earrings, and Serena's long winter coat, her hair swept up into a burgundy felt hat, Miriam felt she blended well into her new neighborhood. She entered a small department store and found gifts for the boys. With her savings from her sales of knitted shawls at the county fair, she bought warm neck scarves for the older boys and a picture book for Teddy.

Along Larimer Street, she stopped to look through the front window of a fine leather goods shop. On display next to expensive handbags was an array of ladies' kid gloves. In instant longing, she stared at those elegant gloves. The only gloves she'd ever worn were cloth. She'd borrowed Serena's today to cover her chapped hands. Someday, she would manage to buy a pair as fine as the ones in the window.

Several businessmen approached, and, glancing up, her eyes met a familiar gaze. The groomed mustache beneath lifted into a smile. Her heart inexplicably picked up a beat. "Mr. Moore," she said, lifting her head a notch.

The gentleman tipped the brim of his dark western hat. "Miss Cole." He slowed his pace as his companions continued on their way. "How nice to see you again." He looked inside the carriage. "And the baby."

Christopher grinned, almost as if he recognized this friendly face, and raised his hand.

Joe Moore's features warmed with obvious affection. "He is a beautiful boy."

"Yes," she said, her voice tinged with pride. "He's my Christmas gift."

Joe angled his head, his dark brows lifting.

"He'll soon become my son. It's a rather unusual situation…."

They began to stroll along the walkway. "Maybe you'd like to talk about it over lunch. I'm on my way to a fine restaurant up the street. Will you join me?"

Her first thought was to say yes, but then she asked boldly, "I would like to, but I must ask, are you married, Mr. Moore?" It would not be proper to dine with a married man.

"No. I'm not."

Did she detect a somber tone in his reply?

"I'm a widower."

"Oh, I'm sorry."

They came toward the middle of the block. A grand hotel rose ahead, at least five stories high. "The restaurant is in the Windsor House. It has wonderful food."

Miriam gaped in amazement. With its elegant architecture and promenade of awnings to the corner, it was like no other building she had ever seen. A group of fashionably dressed men and women mingled at the hotel's main entrance. Her shoes seemed to be bolted to the walkway. "I-I don't know if I'm dressed for the occasion."

Joe Moore's eyes beamed admiration as he placed his hand on her arm. "Miss Cole, you are perfectly dressed for the occasion. I would be honored to have you join me."

With a sudden blush of excitement, Miriam welcomed the warmth of his touch. "Well then, Christopher and I would be honored to join you."

Christmas bells rang out from a nearby church as they entered The Windsor beneath its welcoming porte-cochere.

Later, Miriam would remember the slight pressure of his hand on her arm, the deep tone of his voice guiding her into the grand foyer. The unfamiliar elation of being with an escort...a gentleman. But now, as they entered the expansive hotel dining room, and Joe asked the maitre 'd to seat them, she was aware of an infusion of sights and sounds: sparkling chandeliers and the clinking of silverware on china plates.

After they were seated at a far corner table, and a waiter had poured iced water into crystal goblets, among several goblets set before their plates, Joe asked, "Would you like a glass of wine with lunch?" He held a leather-covered wine menu open, studying it. "I like Port, but when the waiter comes back, he'll probably ask if we'd prefer some fancy French wine that we can't pronounce."

Miriam knew nothing of wines. Her family drank only on holidays, usually a homebrew from one of the neighbors' distilleries. "Please order whatever you like. I don't imbibe spirits much." She lowered her gaze to the polished silverware, hoping Joe Moore wouldn't consider her to be a country rube.

"Well, I don't either, Miss Cole. Coffee suits me just fine."

Joe ordered a luncheon for two of beef medallions in a Sherry mushroom sauce with garden vegetables. Her hunger piqued at the thought of the beef delicacy…and fresh vegetables in December. She pulled a bottle of baby's milk for Christopher from a side pocket of his stroller. When she lifted Christopher from the stroller, he eagerly grasped the bottle with both chubby hands and latched onto it with relish. A potted palm provided some privacy from nearby tables, for which she was grateful.

Leaning toward them, Joe seemed to take an interest in Christopher's obvious enjoyment cooing happily as he drank. Joe had removed his hat, revealing groomed dark hair, a lock of which strayed a little forward over his high forehead. "Please tell me, Miss Cole, how you came to be Christopher's mother."

A warm rush of exhilaration along with a slight apprehension flowed through her. "I can hardly believe it myself. Being his aunt was the most I could have expected until...last week." She hesitated. To share personal family business wasn't something she felt comfortable doing. However, sharing such wonderful news with this charming new acquaintance who smiled warmly at her from across the table came easily. The circumstances she revealed regarding Beth's sad demise from influenza and the sudden revelation of Serena's pregnancy brought an expression of empathy to Joe's intent features.

A new light flickered in his hazel eyes. "From what I see, you'll make a fine mother to Christopher."

Her gaze held his momentarily. "Why, thank you, Mr. Moore." Confidence welled up in her chest as well as a budding attraction she could not deny. "It would be agreeable to me if you'd call me Miriam."

His mustache lifted at the corners into a smile that pleased her. "If you will call me Joe."

"I will, Joe." Her toes curled inside her shoes.

Then Christopher made a little spit-up on the shoulder of her frock before she could pull a towel from the stroller. Embarrassment flushed her cheeks. An observant waiter came over with a napkin and she managed to blot the stain away, and settle the baby back for a nap.

Lunch was served and they heartily ate every bit of the succulent medallions and vegetables on their elegant china plates. She liked his table manners, so different from the men in her family. Always in a hurry, they shoveled food down in greedy gulps and wiped the plates clean with their bread. Joe took his time and dabbed at his mustache frequently with his napkin to catch bits of food. Thankfully, Miriam's mother had taught her how to hold a fork and not to talk with her mouth open.

A faint scar ran between the thumb and forefinger of Joe's right hand up to his wrist. Probably the result of working on his ranch. "Did you say you have a ranch in Kansas?" she asked as they sipped a richly-brewed coffee.

He grinned. "Yep, a cattle ranch."

"I would love to know more about your cattle ranch. I'll bet tending to cattle is much more exciting than harvesting wheat on my family's farm."

He shrugged in a thoughtful way. "Both are necessary to feed a man's family. Cattle are a heck of a lot more stubborn—and loud—than a field of ripe wheat."

She wrinkled her nose. "And smelly?"

He tossed his head back and laughed at her attempt at humor. "Yes, ma'am!"

"Do you have help running your ranch?"

"I do, for sure. My younger brother Will and the foreman keep things going. We hire extra help when we run the herd to Dodge in the spring."

"It takes strong men to manage a ranch, I imagine."

He averted his gaze to the table cloth, his expression clouding. "My wife was a great help, too…before the accident. Things haven't been quite the same without her."

A little chill went down her spine. Did she dare inquire? Curiosity got the better of her. "What accident was she in, may I ask?"

His mouth tightened before he spoke. "One day when we were herding some strays, a snake spooked her horse—and it threw her. She hit her head when she fell…."

Stunned, Miriam felt a sharp pain beneath her breastbone. Her fingers gripped tightly in her lap. "I'm so sorry, Joe."

For a long moment, neither spoke. Miriam took a last sip of her now tepid coffee, thinking the pain of losing a wife or a husband must cut far deeper than losing a sibling.

Joe summoned their waiter to bring the check then turned to her, his features brightening. "I'd like to call for a carriage and take you home, Miriam."

She was flattered and accepted. In the carriage they spoke of the upcoming holiday preparations. How good it was to share it with family. The sound of the horses clopping along the street mingled with the warmth of afternoon sunlight splashing into the carriage windows. Joe's manly tone held her attention; his strong shoulder pressed into hers as they rounded a corner. The edges of his dark mahogany mustache lifted at the corners of his mouth. A man who smiled easily.

For a fleeting moment, she wondered what his mustache would feel like brushing against her upper lip. Prickly or soft? With a slight intake of breath, she

Leslee Breene

straightened her spine, forcing herself to listen to his words rather than fantasize about such worldly temptations.

When they pulled up in front of Kruger's Hardware Store, Miriam caught a glimpse of Serena in the front window. As Joe assisted her and Christopher from the carriage, her sister emerged from inside, brushing wisps of stray hair back into her upswept bun. "Well, is this Mr. Moore? How nice to see you again," she gushed.

Joe greeted Serena with a tip of his hat. "Good day, Mrs. Kruger."

A surge of pride lifted Miriam's spine. "It was a lovely coincidence that we met uptown while I was shopping. Mr. Moore invited Christopher and me to lunch at The Windsor Hotel."

Serena's smile broadened in approval. "How lovely, indeed. Will you join us for a cup of coffee?"

"Thank you, we just had coffee. But I'd sure take a rain check."

Serena's features lit up with spontaneity. "Then, will you join us for Christmas Eve dinner, Mr. Moore?"

Christmas Eve dinner? Miriam's jaw nearly dropped to her knees. The invitation was so…so unexpected.

Joe Moore's mustache lifted slightly, a thoughtful glint reflected in his eyes. "I'm staying with my brother's family and they celebrate Christmas morning…so, it is a possibility. Could I let you know?"

"Of course. Miriam and I will be preparing some old family recipes which I'm sure you'd enjoy. We'll serve dinner at six."

"Yes, ma'am." He boarded the carriage and the driver guided the horses up the street.

Miriam's knees wobbled like cooked spaghetti. "You just invited Joe Moore to Christmas Eve dinner," she said to Serena, her voice rising an octave.

"Well, why not?" She ushered Miriam and the baby inside the store. "Mother always advised taking advantage of a prime opportunity when it presented itself." She winked conspiratorially.

Miriam could recall no such advice. It didn't matter. Her mind was too occupied with the wonderful afterglow of dining with Joe at the Windsor. His enticing nearness in the carriage. The pleasant aroma of his masculine cologne. A bit like cloves. Her feet fairly floated up the stairs.

The following days were a mix of anticipation and dread. Would he come to dinner or not? Was it all too hurried? After all, she hardly knew Joe. And, he would soon be returning to his ranch. Yet each day she found herself watching for the postman, hoping for Joe's reply. Christmas Eve was a mere week away.

On the third morning, an intriguing letter arrived, addressed to *Miss Miriam Cole*. With racing heart, she opened it and was gratified to read the sprawling script accepting Serena's "kind invitation."

Joe Moore's acceptance was cheerfully received by Serena whose morning sickness had finally subsided. Richard, however, quirked a bushy eyebrow at the news and asked, "Joe who?" Richard had his moods,

Miriam had discovered. Not one for small talk or conversation unrelated to store business.

The women set about planning the Christmas dinner, rapidly caught up in shopping and baking. She was glad for the distraction as well as taking care of Christopher's daily needs. He was growing bigger by the week and always easy to amuse.

On the weekend, Richard and the nephews drove their horse wagon up to the foothills and came home with a seven-foot, freshly cut evergreen tree. The piney aroma filled the upper floor as they carried it down the hall and into the family parlor. Her brother-in-law was a good father, Miriam had to admit. After setting up the tree near a front window, favorite ornaments were retrieved from a large box, and everyone found one to hang on a wide branch. Popcorn and cranberry chains were strung from top to bottom. The older boys helped Teddy up a step ladder to hang a shiny ball that he had covered with crimson foil. Richard climbed the ladder to anchor a painted gold star on the top.

Admiring their efforts from across the room, Serena added a hand-carved nativity crèche to the fireplace mantel. "We'll light some Christmas candles for the tree on Christmas Eve."

"Why can't we light the candles today, Mommy?" Teddy asked with urgency, his blond mop in need of combing.

Serena caressed his upturned cheek. "Because it's too early. The candles are to honor the baby Jesus on his special night."

Teddy groaned, his small shoulders drooping.

"And we don't want to risk burning the house

down...." Serena whispered to Miriam. Lighted candles on a Christmas tree caused many fires over the holidays.

Miriam bent over Teddy. "Let's go make some hot cocoa to warm up you boys after your hard work in that cold snow."

"Cocoa!" the boys chorused in response. A swift stampede raced ahead of Miriam on the way to the kitchen.

🎄🎄🎄

Christmas Eve, with all of its promise and preparation, had arrived. The ivory lace table cloth, inherited from Grandmother Cole, adorned the dining room table. The family's best crystal and china, and cloth napkins set upon it. Everything sparkled beneath the overhead brass chandelier and its lit candle globes.

Miriam observed the seven chairs, the added highchair for Christopher, the evergreen and holly centerpiece. Had she forgotten anything? Where should Joe be seated? She wanted him to be near her but also close to Richard so the men could get acquainted.

"Come help me finish the punch," Serena called from the kitchen. Oh yes, the eggnog punch! "Taste it and see if it has enough brandy." Serena held out a long-handled spoon to Miriam for a sip. "This is elegant...even if I imagine the men would like more. I like it mild," Miriam said.

From the large oven, the aroma of roasting turkey and sweet potatoes filled the room. The cranberry sauce was already in the ice box. Miriam placed the rich nog next to it. When it was time, they would pour it into the crystal punch bowl and everyone would gather 'round the dining room table for a toast. The children, not allowed spirits, would enjoy a sweet milk punch.

A short time later, the family mingled in the parlor as the skies darkened outside. Everyone was groomed and dressed in their Christmas finery. Miriam wore a frock of claret velveteen and Serena wore one of forest green. Richard, in his Sunday suit, and the boys in theirs, began the holiday ritual of lighting the candles attached to the tree. He climbed the ladder and carefully lit each one.

The grandfather clock in the hallway struck half past five which made Miriam jump. She carried Christopher to the front window and gazed out at the street. A light snow had started to fall, glistening below the corner street light. Would Joe arrive early?

After awhile, the nephews became energetic and started playing tag around the dining room table. Serena persuaded them to cease and asked Miriam to start a quiet game around the fireplace. At quarter to six, she left them to feed Christopher his bottle. The clock chimed again at six o'clock. Where was Joe?

"I hope our dinner guest hasn't gotten lost," Richard muttered loud enough for her to hear as she passed him on the way to the kitchen. A discomforting cramp gripped her stomach and would not let go.

"Do you need any help?" Miriam asked Serena who was bending over the open oven door.

"No, I'm just basting broth over the turkey to keep

it moist."

Once again energetic, and after complaining of their hunger, the nephews chased out in the hall, resuming their game of tag. Miriam hovered near the front window, worrying over Joe's arrival. Could he have forgotten the time of dinner? The Krugers were always prompt.

"I'm having some of that eggnog," Richard announced and went to help himself. Serena admonished him for his impatience, but even she appeared a bit concerned as the minutes lengthened.

Finally, a horse pulling a covered rig rounded the corner and trotted up the street. Miriam's pulse raced when it slowed in front of the store. The driver was wearing a western-brimmed hat. "I think it's Joe," she called, her voice tinged with anticipation.

When someone knocked loudly on the front door, Miriam was halfway down the hall. Richard came up behind her. "I'll answer it, just to be sure." She and the boys followed close behind.

A gusty cold wind swept into the room when Richard opened the door. Joe, dressed in long black coat and a knapsack on his back, stepped inside. Before he could remove his hat, Teddy was at his side. "Are you Santa Claus?" he asked tentatively.

Joe smiled at Miriam and patted the top of Teddy's blond head. "No, son, I'm just his helper."

"You're late," came the greeting from another nephew.

Richard stuck out his hand and Miriam introduced the men, tamping down a twinge of embarrassment for Joe.

"Sorry to be late, folks." Joe glanced down at the boys. "I had to feed my horse some oats before I hitched him up."

"We're going to eat turkey," Teddy announced as they all headed up the back stairs where the aroma of their roasting dinner permeated the hallway.

After Miriam helped Joe off with his long coat and hat, he touched her arm briefly, the light from the fireplace reflecting in his eyes. "You're looking very pretty this evening." The unexpected compliment left her nearly speechless. "Thank you," she managed in a lowered voice.

Serena invited Joe to join them at the punch bowl for a Christmas toast. Shortly after, the family was seated at the laden dining room table and the women served steaming platters from the kitchen. "The turkey doesn't look too burnt," Richard commented as he stood and lifted the silver handled knife in preparation to begin his annual carving duties.

Serena shot him an irritated look. "It's a well crisped bird...and we should be thankful we have such fine company to share it with," she said, nodding to Joe. "Shall we take a moment to give thanks? I'll be glad to say the grace."

Richard contritely set the knife down and bowed his head as the rest of the family lowered their gaze to the tablecloth. When Serena finished, Christopher tapped his spoon on the highchair tray and grinned up at Miriam. "Let's eat then," the older nephew enthused.

And they did. Heartily.

The dinner met all of Miriam's expectations. Serena was an accomplished cook, and she had contributed her own cooking skills. Ivory candles in their polished brass holders glowed amidst the silk poinsettia centerpiece as well as in the chandelier above. The Kansas gentleman across the table from her was obviously enjoying his dinner, accepting two helpings of everything. "Thank you, ma'am," he would say every time Serena served him, his deep voice surrounding Miriam with a sense of wellbeing.

While coffee was brewing in the kitchen, Richard made a point of querying Joe about his ranch near Great Bend. It pleased Miriam to hear that the ranch was quite large and supported hundreds of cattle. Joe's parents had passed away and left Joe as majority owner, his brothers inheriting other land acreage.

The nephews were excused from the table and congregated around the tree, eyeing the large knapsack beneath it. "Would you boys like to have a look at what's inside?" Joe asked, a knowing twinkle in his eyes. If your dad approves."

"Can we, Father?" the boys chimed together.

"Bring the knapsack to Mr. Moore and let him show you," Richard instructed.

With delight, the family watched Joe Moore open his bag of surprises. He retrieved boxes of oranges and nuts. Belgian chocolates for Serena and Miriam.

"Christmas crackers!" someone exclaimed when Joe lifted out the last gift. Miriam bounced Christopher on her knee wondering what they were. She didn't have to wait long to find out. The box was torn open and eager hands grasped the colorful log-shaped toys. When two boys played tug-of-war with a toy, it would snap apart, releasing sugared almonds and a paper message of good luck. The cracking sound was met with exuberant laughter. Fun for the boys but frightening to Christopher. Miriam excused herself and took the baby off to bed.

"Miriam, come have some cake!" Serena called from the parlor. Miriam tucked blankets around Christopher asleep in his crib, kissed his warm cheek and went to join the ongoing festivities.

The Christmas cake was Serena's crowning achievement: two layers filled with currants and pecans, seasoned with Sherry and nutmeg. Holly sprigs and red berries decorated the white icing on the top. "Our grandmother's recipe," she said as she offered Joe a large slice on the family's gold-trimmed china. Joe smiled broadly. "It smells wonderful, ma'am."

Although she had helped Serena make the cake, a twinge of jealousy surprised Miriam when she saw Joe devour it. She would copy the recipe and make it herself one day. There was much she needed to learn about pleasing a man. At least, she'd baked an apple raisin fruit bread for Joe to take home to his family.

After the women cleared the dishes from the table and took them to the kitchen to soak in the big metal sink, they returned to the parlor. Richard put more logs on the fire, which made the room alight with an amber glow. The boys gathered around an upright piano near the fireplace. "Will you play some songs for us, Mama?"

Serena nodded. "It wouldn't be Christmas without our music." She seated herself on the piano bench and began to play the traditional hymns, carried down from one generation to the next. Voices raised in unison. "Oh, Come All Ye Faithful," was followed by other favorites. Joe and Miriam stood behind Serena. His deep tenor mingled with the boys' higher tones. Once she felt his hand lightly placed at her waist. Her gaze found his reflected in the firelight, and her heart fluttered.

A muffled boyish giggle preceded a nudge at her opposite elbow. The older nephew waved something green between her and Joe. "Grownups are supposed to kiss under the mistletoe," he announced boldly. Teddy jumped up and down with glee. "Kiss her, kiss her."

A rush of heat flooded Miriam's face and neck. She could throttle those boys!

"That's enough," Richard interrupted, sending the perpetrator a glare.

Serena closed the piano lid over the keys. "It's bedtime."

Even though Miriam would have liked the evening to never end, she sighed in relief at her sister's pronouncement. Barely able to look at Joe, she did glance his way and caught the amused reaction in the lift of his mustache. Then she, too, had to tamp down an urge to chuckle at the boys' childish ploy. Mistletoe, indeed.

"Remember," Serena said, "We get up early tomorrow morning to see what Santa Claus has brought you—and, we mustn't be late for church."

Spontaneous responses of enthusiasm erupted at the mention of "Santa Claus."

"Thank Mr. Moore for his generous gifts," Serena added, attempting to herd the trio toward the hallway.

They all were unanimous with their replies of gratitude.

Joe shook hands with Richard. "Thank you all for this grand evening. It was very special to me."

"I will see you to the front door," Miriam offered and hurried to snatch her winter shawl from the hall closet. Out on the street, a veil of snow drifted quietly beneath the street light. The horse and rig were frosted with white like snow statues. Plumes of steam rose from the steed's nostrils into the night air.

Miriam drew her shawl more snuggly around her shoulders. "We were so happy you could join us for Christmas," she said, looking up into Joe's eyes, shaded beneath his western brim.

"I assure you, the pleasure was all mine, Miss Miriam," he said and moved closer to her. She didn't know if she should shake his gloved hand or...what was the proper thing to do? His manly presence made her suddenly shy.

He cupped her chin gently with a tender touch and lifted it a notch. In the next moment, she felt the light brush of his mustache against her upper lip and the softness of his lips on hers. *He was kissing her.* A sweet kiss in the gently falling snow. Her whole being was filled with light, and stars, and an unexplainable longing. Kisses in her life had been few, especially romantic kisses. No one had ever kissed her with such command mixed with tenderness.

Their arms went around each other in what seemed a most natural embrace. "Dear Miriam," he murmured in her ear, "we don't need mistletoe." As he pulled back slightly, he said, "Come visit me at the ranch this spring. Bring Christopher with you."

"Come visit you at your ranch?" Had she heard him correctly?

His grin was irresistible. "Late spring is the best time to come when the new calves are just finding their footing."

The image of bawling little heifers tagging close to their mother cows made her smile. Christopher would just be taking his first steps then.

Joe took her hands in his, warming them against the cold. "Mrs. Dolan, our cook, will take care of all your needs. And, she loves children."

Mrs. Dolan would placate Richard's disapproval of Miriam's traveling and staying on Joe's ranch without a chaperone. "I could come back before Serena's baby arrives," she said, thinking aloud, a spark of enthusiasm kindled within her.

Joe held her hands firmly for one last minute. Then he picked up his knapsack, now filled with Miriam's apple and raisin bread and ginger cookies from Serena, untethered the horse, and climbed inside the covered rig. The horse shook his frosty mane and gave an impatient whinny. Touching his gloved hand to his hat brim, Joe called, "I'll be writing you soon. Merry Christmas!"

"Merry Christmas!"

Miriam watched the rig pull away down the street. She stepped back into the shelter of the lighted doorway, hugging herself in the crisp evening air. From a nearby church, bells chimed. So many gifts were hers: Christopher, her family, Joe.

Indeed, the gift of love was the best gift of all.

The End

Amazon Top Ten
YA short fiction ebook, 2014

JOURNEY TO SAND CASTLE EXCERPT
CHAPTER ONE

Monday, August 29, 2005

Wailing wolves—that was the sound of it. Then louder—like a mammoth jet hovering in the turbulent skies. *Katrina.*

Tess Cameron stood riveted behind a boarded window of her empty Jefferson Elementary School classroom. Peering through a crack in the boards, she saw ragged rooftops and debris hurled through the streets. A shattering sound from the floor above her sent chills along her arms. Shards of glass whipped past the window like jagged missiles.

Showing no mercy, torrents of rain beat down from the angry sky. She imagined other parts of the city near the levees where flood waters would climb quickly to heights above a man's head. Her skin flushed clammy to the touch. Her legs went weak beneath her.

How high would flood waters climb here? She didn't know how to swim. Fear pumped her heart like a sledge hammer until it felt like it might pump right out of her chest.

Hours later, a gray watery silence smothered the city.

* * *

Tuesday, August 30

Tess rubbed her eyes, gritty from lack of sleep, and faced the tide of new evacuees streaming into Jefferson's gymnasium. Wet and bedraggled, their bodies as well as their spirits were devastated by the deluge. Masks of anxiety covered their faces. Now homeless and separated from their families, they had nowhere else to go for shelter but here.

It was a miracle the two-story school was intact. Perhaps because it was built of brick, built to withstand strong winds. Although all types of litter covered the grounds and several windows on the second floor were shattered, the interior had not been flooded.

When she'd arrived Sunday afternoon, offering what aid she could give to her neighbors and young students, Tess had had no idea Hurricane Katrina would leave such destruction behind. But then, just beginning her second year in the New Orleans area, what would she know about hurricanes? A former Air Force brat, she only recalled survival skills which involved adapting to wherever her family was transferred around the globe.

"Can you help us?" A young woman with disheveled brown hair and haunted eyes hurried toward her, a toddler straddling one hip. On her heels followed two young boys and a small, almond-skinned girl. There was something familiar about the girl.

"Over here." Tess pointed to cots set up against a gymnasium wall. "You can have these. There are blankets and some snacks for the children."

The woman's face crumpled. "My cousin is missing—her car was washed away. Can y'all get any information about her?"

"I'm sorry. We haven't been able to contact the local authorities yet. You know the power's out"— Tess stopped in mid-sentence. A rambling explanation would not make this anxious woman's situation any better. "What is your cousin's name and address?" She slipped a ballpoint pen from her clipboard. "I'll pass it along as soon as I can."

"It's her mother, Carrie Pearl," the woman said in a low voice, referring to the small girl with large, red-rimmed eyes who hovered behind her. "They've been livin' with us until she could find a place."

A strange tingle darted along Tess's spine as she jotted down the information. "Carrie's a teacher here at Jefferson, isn't she?"

"Yeah. That's her girl, Crystal. She doesn't know what happened." The woman shifted the toddler in her arms. "I haven't told her yet. I don't know how to tell her."

Although Tess didn't know Carrie well, her reaction to the bedraggled child now climbing onto one of the cots was one of immediate sympathy.

"And what is your name?"

"Winona Bingham. My husband's in Houston lookin' for a job." She glanced around at her two boys, their grim faces revealing the nightmare they'd lived through. "I wish we could have got out with him, before the storm hit."

"I can understand that." Tess set the clipboard down on a folding chair and passed a few bags of chips to the hungry children.

The toddler on Winona's hip, scantily clad in T-shirt and diapers, began to whine, grasping at her mother's arm. "Do y'all have any baby formula?" Near desperation tinged Winona Bingham's request. "All I had time to bring was a few diapers and a change of clothes."

The agony of what this mother had suffered was one more notch on a belt of misery, her plight similar to other evacuees Tess had talked to during the last twenty-four hours. They had lost everything. "We don't have baby food. But we do have some bottled water back in the locker room. Wait here."

Taking up her clipboard, Tess maneuvered through the crowd of arrivals to the locker room at the rear of the gym. "Carrie Pearl is lost in the flood," she told the assistant principal, John Lincoln, a usually jovial black man in his late thirties.

John's lower lip curled downward. "No way. Carrie's a teacher upstairs in the music department."

Tess shook her head in dismay. "Her cousin just came in with her three kids and Carrie's little girl."

"Geez. That's tough. Keep a list and we'll turn it over to the police…whenever we can reach them. All the lines are down. The cell phones don't work." John's dark-eyed gaze roamed the room while several volunteers rationed food supplies, salvaged from the school cafeteria, to take back to the gym. "Hey, remember that stuff is scarce as hen's teeth. Make it last."

Tess reached for four bottles from a locker. "How's the water holding out?"

John raked a hand through short black hair, sweat beading his upper lip. "Not much left. And there's no way to run over to the market for more with flood water up to your elbows."

A knowing sigh escaped her. "I've got to locate some baby formula."

His shoulders sagged. "Haven't seen any. I'll keep my eyes open."

"Thanks, John." Carrying her precious water bottles, Tess returned to the gym and its occupants rife with grief and uncertainty. No food, no power, no running water. A roof overhead and a cot was all the school had to offer.

And, from the looks of the crowded gymnasium, available cots were running short fast.

Leslee Breene

CHAPTER TWO

Thursday, September 1

Morning came early. Launching her body into action on the fourth day, without the customary shower and cup of coffee taken for granted in her former life, Tess entered the bustling gymnasium. Occupants were grabbing up their meager possessions. A ragged line of people moved toward the school's front entrance.

To the side of the gym, an elderly man wearing a flimsy bathrobe slumped in his wheel chair. Her breath quickening, Tess hurried over to him and pressed fingers below the man's ear, seeking a pulse. And found none.

She craned her neck toward the entrance where National Guardsmen were in view. "I've got an emergency!" she hollered to one of them.

Realizing her CPR experience was rusty, Tess leaned over to the man's face. His features hung drooped, mouth open. His chest was still, his skin cool to the touch. A terrible dread swept over her. It was no use.

A tall, red-haired Guardsman appeared within seconds, repeated the search for a pulse, couldn't find one, and proclaimed the man deceased. In a rush, he pushed the wheelchair away.

Tess stood in the middle of the gymnasium, her mind swimming like a fish trying to escape an undercurrent. Voices and colors surrounding her melted together. *I've got to focus, pull myself together.*

Houston. Wasn't this group going to Houston? Winona Bingham and her family would be headed there. She must catch her before she left. Say goodbye and wish them well.

Shaking off the temporary shock of the evacuee's untimely death, she moved toward the line of people in the front of the gym.

She looked for Winona, searching the haggard faces of women with children. Dark, shoulder-length hair, medium height, holding a year-old toddler. Two boys and a girl. So many mothers; so many children. No match.

Buses waited outside. People boarding. Which one would Winona be on? Wouldn't she have tried to seek out Tess before she left? No. Not enough time.

If I just had a cup of coffee. Some orange juice.

Out of breath, she stopped and leaned against a wall near the entrance. Sweat dampened her brow and upper lip. Absently she swiped at her forehead, pulled fingers through her short, dark, oily hair. Her reflection in the large side window scared her. An eerie phantom stared back into her eyes.

Other evacuees milled around in haphazard groups. Maybe Winona hadn't left yet. Maybe more buses would arrive later for Houston.

Impulsively Tess swerved back into the gym. It seemed important that she at least say goodbye to Winona and her clan. They had bonded during these last days, sharing the conversations of women, even though their lives were totally dissimilar.

She made her way to the rear side wall where the Binghams had stayed. Her hopes fell when she saw their empty cots. Then rose when she caught sight of little Crystal sitting with her legs dangling over the far cot. But as she came closer, her gut told her something wasn't right.

The child was sobbing, heart-wrenching sobs that shook her body and wrenched Tess's heart.

"Crystal." Tess sat down next to her. "Where's Winona?"

The child shook her head, misery etched on her tear-stained face. "Don't know…."

Bewildered, Tess slipped one arm around her then glanced down at a folded piece of paper pinned to Crystal's blue T-shirt. "Here, let me see this." She removed the pin and unfolded the paper. Out fell a billfold-size photo of Crystal and Carrie, and a ten dollar bill. Hastily she read the scrawled note, her vision blurring, a hot ember burning in her chest.

Tess,
Sorry—we can't afford to keep Crystal with us.
She likes you. She is a good little girl.

*Call her grandpa in Sand Castle, Co. He's her only
living kin. Jud Pearl—c/o Jud's Tobacco Shop.
God bless you, Winona*

Tess gaped at the note then at the orphaned child next to her. Left behind like a stray puppy—with little more than the dirty clothes on her back.

We can't afford to keep Crystal with us.

Crystal looked up at her, tears glistening in her wide topaz eyes, and hiccupped. "Where's my mommy?"

The earth careened on its axis, out of control. A tightness gathered in Tess's throat. How in the world could she tell this sweet child that her mommy was gone, lost in the flood?

Tess took a shaky breath, tears welling in her own eyes. Holding Crystal close, she said, "I don't know, honey. But I do know she loves you…." Her voice cracked. "Very much."

"I want her. I want my mommy."

Tess gently wiped the child's face and running nose with the corner of a blanket, looked into eyes of innocence and trust. Stunned at her sudden dilemma, she reflected on her previous wandering past. She had only been responsible for herself then. Conflicting emotions tumbled through her mind.

Did she have a choice? Really?

Tess wrapped her arms around Crystal's small shoulders. Whatever troubles awaited her, she could not abandon this little soul.

For now, all they had was each other.

Journey to Sand Castle is available in soft cover and eBook. To visit the book's page, use the link below.

https://www.amazon.com/Journey-Sand-Castle-Leslee-Breene/dp/1484958977/ref

To enjoy more of my stories, visit my author page on Amazon.com at:

https://www.amazon.com/Leslee-Breene/e/B001JP2DTQ/ref=dp_byline_cont_book_1

Leslee Breene

ABOUT THE AUTHOR

Leslee Breene, award-winning author of novel and short fiction, takes pride in being a Denver native. She lives beneath the Colorado Rockies with her husband and, hopefully soon, a beloved rescue canine. Her love of animals is obvious in the secondary character roles they play in her books.

Ms. Breene attended the University of Denver, received a Denver Fashion Group Scholarship, and graduated from the Fashion Institute of Technology, New York City. For several years, she worked as a newspaper fashion illustrator in San Francisco.

During leisure time away from the computer, she enjoys scouting for book settings with her husband in the Colorado Rockies. Some memorable research sites are Leadville, the Sangre de Cristo Mountains, the Colorado Sand Dunes, and Jackson Hole, Wyoming.

Ms. Breene is an active member of Colorado Romance Writers, Romance Writers of America, and Women Writing the West.

She is available for Denver/suburban area library and group speaking engagements. She welcomes visitors at her website: http://www.lesleebreene.com and https://www.facebook.com/author.lesleebreene.